BREAKING *the* CHAIN

FAITH, HOPE, AND HEALING
IN THE FACE OF FAMILY VIOLENCE

Dr. ANTONIO R. PAIZ

Sagga Publishing House LLC

Sagga Publishing House LLC, March 2025

Copyright © 2025 by Dr. Antonio R. Paiz

Premium Mass-Market Paperback ISBN: 978-1-964642-17-8

Premium Mass-Market Hardback: 978-1-964642-18-5

eBook ISBN: 978-1-964642-19-2

Library of Congress Control Number: 2025903783

Published in the United States by Sagga Publishing House LLC, Texas.

Printed in the United States of America.

Acknowledgments

First and foremost, I want to give all glory to the Lord for the transformative work He has done in my life and the lives of my family. Through the truth of the Holy Bible, I have come to understand the profound depths of His love, grace, and wisdom. This journey has been enriched by exploring the beliefs, religions, and cultures of others, providing me with a broader perspective and a deeper appreciation of the Word. These experiences have shaped not only my faith but also this work, which stands as a testament to His enduring truth.

I am deeply grateful to the visionary leadership and guidance of the directors at Vision International University in Escondido, California. Their dedication to equipping others for the work of the Lord has been a source of inspiration and encouragement throughout this process.

To my beloved wife, Josephine: your unwavering, godly love and steadfast support have been my rock. Your faith and encouragement have carried me through this journey, and I am forever grateful to you. To my beautiful family: thank you for your love, patience, and belief in me. You are my greatest blessings.

A heartfelt thank you to Sagga Publishing House LLC for bringing this work to life. Your support, professionalism, and commitment to excellence have been invaluable. This book would not have been possible without your partnership.

Finally, to the readers of this work: may it inspire you to seek truth, grow in understanding, and reflect on the profound role of faith in our lives. This book is my offering, born of personal experience, knowledge, and the doctrine of God's Word. To Him be all the glory.

Thank you all.

Preface

Family violence is not merely a personal tragedy; it is a societal crisis affecting countless families across all cultures, socioeconomic statuses, and faiths. Despite decades of awareness campaigns, prevention strategies, and intervention programs, the problem continues to grow, shattering lives and communities in its wake. Why? Because we are leaving something crucial out—something powerful, transformative, and deeply healing.

In our well-intentioned efforts to create inclusive, non-judgmental safe spaces, we have often excluded one of the most potent resources available: spiritual guidance. The Bible, a source of wisdom for billions around the world, offers profound teachings on love, respect, forgiveness, and unity—all foundational elements for building healthy families and healing broken ones. Yet, in many places where families seek refuge and guidance—such as shelters, schools, and government agencies—spiritual counsel is frequently omitted, sometimes out of fear of infringing on individual rights or appearing biased.

However, the absence of faith-based support leaves a void for those whose cultural and spiritual beliefs are integral to their identity and healing process. By excluding this resource, we may be inadvertently hindering their journey to recovery.

Through my experiences as a volunteer and my work with the San Antonio Police Department's Family Assistance Crisis Team, I have witnessed firsthand the devastating cycles of anger, fear, and pain that perpetuate family violence. Yet, I have also seen the transformative power of love, faith, and community in breaking those cycles. I have watched broken families find restoration, individuals regain hope, and communities come together to support each other through the power of faith.

This book seeks to bridge the gap by integrating biblical teachings with practical, real-world solutions for preventing and healing family violence. It does not seek to impose religious beliefs or alienate those of different faiths or no faith at all. Rather, it offers a source of hope, wisdom, and strength for those who seek it.

The goal of this book is simple but profound: to inspire transformation. It aims to provide comfort and healing to families who feel broken and to offer tools for building healthier, more loving relationships. It calls for a more holistic approach to family violence—one that integrates spiritual guidance with community support and legal intervention.

If you are reading this, it means you care—about your family, your community, or perhaps your own journey of healing. Know this: there is hope, there is healing, and there is a way forward. This book is here to guide you on that journey.

Introduction

Domestic violence is not just a personal issue; it is a social, economic, and political crisis with far-reaching implications for public health and community well-being. It affects not only the physical and mental health of over 20% of women at some point in their lives but also the emotional and psychological health of their children. Children who witness domestic violence often carry deep emotional scars that shape their behavior, relationships, and worldview. If left unaddressed, this trauma can perpetuate a cycle of violence that echoes across generations.

Despite increasing awareness and evolving approaches to domestic violence, the problem remains overwhelming. Families are torn apart, relationships shattered, and communities weakened. We are witnessing an escalation in family violence—brother against sister, parent against child, spouse against spouse. The damage is profound, affecting every aspect of society.

When I first became involved with the domestic violence movement in 1995, volunteering with the San Antonio Police Department's Family Assistance Crisis Team, I saw the devastating impact up close. I witnessed women trapped in fear, children scarred by trauma, and men haunted by cycles of anger and shame. I also saw the limitations of our current systems. In many cases, victims needed more than just a safe space—they needed healing, guidance, and hope. They needed a path not just to survive but to rebuild.

Through my experiences, I came to realize that our approach to domestic violence is incomplete. While public health interventions, legal protections, and community support systems are crucial, they are not enough. Many victims, especially those from faith-based communities, seek deeper healing and restoration—a journey that involves not just emotional recovery but also spiritual renewal.

This book proposes a holistic approach that integrates biblical teachings with practical strategies for preventing and healing domestic violence. It explores how the Bible's teachings on love, respect, forgiveness, and reconciliation can offer guidance and comfort to those affected by family violence. This approach is not about imposing religious beliefs but about offering spiritual resources for those who seek them. It is about creating a space for healing that respects individual faith journeys and cultural contexts.

Why include faith?

Because faith is powerful. It offers hope, strength, and courage. It provides a moral framework that can inspire change, healing, and reconciliation. It can break the chains of shame, guilt, and fear that often bind victims and perpetrators alike. But most importantly, it offers a pathway to forgiveness and peace.

This book does not claim that faith alone is the solution, nor does it minimize the need for legal protection, psychological support, and community intervention. Rather, it argues that faith-based guidance can complement these solutions, providing a more comprehensive and compassionate approach to healing.

To those affected by domestic violence:

Know that your pain is real, your journey is valid, and your healing is possible. There is hope, there is healing, and there is a way forward. You are not alone. This book is here to guide you on that journey.

Contents

Chapter 1

The Emotional Labyrinth of Abuse

"The human heart was never meant to carry such heavy burdens. Yet, in the shadows of abuse, it learns to endure by constructing walls, weaving illusions, and splitting the abuser into two faces—the one who loves and the one who shatters.

But hear this: You are not broken. You are not weak. You are healing. With every tear that falls, with every breath you take, you are reclaiming the life that was always yours. You are piecing together the fragments of your soul, rediscovering your strength, and stepping into the light that has always been within you.

You are not just surviving. You are rising."

-Dr. Antonio R. Paiz

The Illusion of Duality: Loving the Abuser and Surviving the Abuse

Victims of domestic violence live in a state of emotional contradiction. They learn to separate the abuser from the abuse, to compartmentalize their pain. They see two people: the one who compliments them and the one who degrades them, the one who says, "I love you," and the one who says, "You're worthless."

This psychological divide is not weakness—it is survival. When the abuser's love is the only love they know, they cling to the good moments, even when they are surrounded by fear. They rationalize the cruelty, excusing the hurtful words, the violent outbursts, because the person they love is still in there somewhere, buried beneath the anger.

But this separation, this illusion, is dangerous. It keeps victims trapped, convincing them to stay, to hope, to forgive, even when the cycle of violence shows no signs of ending.

The Dangerous Illusion

When victims separate the abuser from the abuse, they do so to preserve hope, to hold on to the possibility of change. They convince themselves that if they can just be better—more obedient, more understanding, more loving—the "good" person will remain, and the "bad" one will disappear.

But this cycle only deepens the wound. Each act of forgiveness is met with another betrayal, each act of love with another dose of cruelty. The emotional confusion is paralyzing. Victims begin to doubt themselves, questioning their own worth, their own sanity.

"Am I really that difficult? Maybe I deserved it. Maybe if I just try harder…"

This self-doubt is reinforced by the abuser, who manipulates reality, making the victim feel responsible for the violence. "Look what you made me do." "You always push me to this."

The abuser's words echo in their minds, feeding their guilt, trapping them in a cycle of shame and fear. The line between love and hate blurs, until they can no longer tell the difference.

Living in Fear and Isolation

Abuse is not just physical; it is emotional, psychological, and spiritual. It isolates the victim, breaking down their support systems until they feel utterly alone. They are taught not to trust anyone, not even themselves.

They are afraid to reach out for help, afraid to expose their pain, afraid of judgment and disbelief. They are afraid to trust, because trust has been weaponized against them.

This isolation is compounded by a culture of silence. Neighbors hear the shouting, the breaking glass, the cries for help, but they turn away. "It's not my business." "I don't want to get involved." This silence is complicity, and it reinforces the victim's sense of abandonment.

Family violence is not a private matter. It affects the community, the children who hear every insult and every blow, and the souls who carry the weight of this pain in silence. We cannot afford to stand on the sidelines.

The Complexity of Leaving

"Why don't they just leave?" It's a question often asked by those who have never been trapped in the cycle of abuse. But leaving is not as simple as walking out the door. It is terrifying, complicated, and fraught with danger.

Victims know that leaving can escalate the violence. They know that the abuser may hunt them down, stalking them at work, harassing their friends and family, waiting outside their child's school.

Research shows that the most dangerous time for a victim is when they try to leave. It is then that the abuser feels the loss of control and becomes most unpredictable, most violent.

The Role of Faith and Support

In moments of despair, when hope seems impossible, faith can be a lifeline. "I can do all things through Christ who strengthens me." (Philippians 4:13) These words remind victims that they are not alone, that there is a power greater than the fear that binds them.

But faith alone is not enough. Victims need support—practical, emotional, and spiritual. They need a community that listens, believes, and acts. They need safe spaces, trusted friends, and guidance from trained professionals who understand the complexity of abuse.

Faith-based communities have a unique role to play. They can offer counseling, prayer, and spiritual healing. But they must also provide practical support, helping victims find shelters, legal assistance, and financial independence.

The Escape from Despair

In a world where violence is a daily reality, escape can feel impossible. Many victims turn to drugs or alcohol, seeking an escape from the nightmare. But the high is fleeting, the pain returns, and the cycle of abuse continues.

Some consider running away, others contemplate suicide. They feel trapped, hopeless, convinced that they are alone. But they are not. There is a way out. There is hope. There is healing.

Reaching out for help is terrifying, but it is the first step to freedom. It requires courage, trust, and faith. Faith in oneself, faith in others, and faith in God.

"Come unto me, all ye that labor and are heavy laden, and I will give you rest." (Matthew 11:28)

Breaking the Cycle of Silence

We must break the cycle of silence. We must become a society that listens, believes, and acts. Domestic violence is not just a private issue; it is a public health crisis. It affects us all—our communities, our workplaces, our schools.

We must become the voice for those who are voiceless, the strength for those who feel powerless. We must offer safety, support, and hope.

A Call to Action

If you know someone who is suffering, don't turn away. Listen. Believe them. Offer support without judgment. Guide them to resources—shelters, hotlines, counselors, and faith-based support systems. Let them know that they are not alone.

If you are a victim, reach out. There is no shame in seeking help. There is no weakness in wanting freedom. You are loved. You are worthy of safety, respect, and happiness.

And if you are a leader in a faith community, embrace your responsibility. Offer not only prayer and spiritual guidance but also practical resources and referrals. Work with local organizations, shelters, and counselors. Become a safe haven for those in need.

Hope, Healing, and Freedom

Breaking free from abuse is not easy. It is a journey of courage, healing, and faith. It requires breaking down the walls of shame, rebuilding trust, and rediscovering hope.

But it is possible. Through community, faith, and love, the cycle of violence can be broken. Hearts can be healed, lives restored, and hope renewed.

"And ye shall know the truth, and the truth shall make you free." (John 8:32)

Let us stand together, in faith and love, and bring light to the darkness. Let us break the cycle of silence. Let us fight for justice, for healing, and for hope.

For there is no darkness that cannot be overcome by light.

Chapter 2

The Silent Reality of Children Growing Up in Domestic Violence

"Children know the sound of every blow, the vibration of every wall as their mother's body hits it, and the pitch of every raised voice. At some point, those children lie in their beds, crying, praying—if they even have the words for prayers—begging for the fighting to stop."

-Dr. Antonio R. Paiz

Growing up with Domestic Violence

This is the silent reality of children who grow up in homes marked by domestic violence. Their innocence is shattered, replaced with a constant state of fear and anxiety. They learn to tiptoe around tension, to read the warning signs in a parent's face, to recognize the shifting tones that signal the next outburst of violence.

In these homes, childhood is stolen. Laughter is muffled by the echoes of shouting, and playtime is overshadowed by the dread of what might happen next. These children become masters of survival, learning to be invisible, to make themselves small and quiet, hoping to avoid becoming the next target of anger. They grow up far too quickly, carrying burdens far too heavy for their small shoulders.

They grow up in a world where love and pain are intertwined, where safety is a fleeting illusion. Home, which should be a place of comfort and security, becomes a place of fear and instability. The walls themselves seem to whisper fear, holding the memories of slammed doors, broken glass, and shattered trust. The air is heavy with anger, sorrow, and unspoken secrets, suffocating the hope and innocence that should fill a child's heart.

For many children, this is not just a memory; it is their reality—a cycle that continues day after day, night after night. They wake up wondering if today will be peaceful or if they will once again witness the terrifying transformation of someone they love into someone they fear. They go to bed praying for silence, for calm, for safety.

A Childhood in the Crossfire

To understand the impact of domestic violence on children, we must first confront the harsh truth: growing up in a violent home is like living in a war zone. The effects are profound, complex, and long-lasting. Children are not merely witnesses; they are victims. They internalize the violence, blaming themselves, feeling powerless, and growing up far too quickly.

Consider Rosemary's story. As a child, she watched her father's explosive anger tear through their home. Her mother's attempts to placate him were futile, her fear palpable. Rosemary hated her father, not just for his fists but for the way he made her mother shrink into herself, her spirit breaking piece by piece.

As Hong (1994) writes, *To grow up in a home where one parent abuses the other is to live in a suspended state of terror"* (p. 51).

Rosemary's childhood was not defined by laughter or joy but by the sounds of arguments echoing off the walls, by the vibration of the floor as her father's rage reverberated through the house. This constant state of fear and hyper-vigilance leaves deep emotional scars. These children are at risk of developing anxiety, depression, and post-traumatic stress disorder. They may struggle with feelings of guilt and shame, believing, in their innocence, that they are somehow to blame for the violence. The impact on their self-esteem is profound, leading them to doubt their worth and question their place in the world.

The effects are not just emotional but also behavioral. These children may become withdrawn, avoiding friendships and social interactions out of fear of revealing their painful secret. Others may act out in anger or rebellion, mirroring the violence they have witnessed. They may struggle academically, finding it difficult to concentrate when their minds are preoccupied with fear and worry.

The Promises They Make to Themselves

In the darkness, alone with their tears, children of violence make silent vows:

- "I will never marry."

- "I will never hurt anyone the way I've been hurt."

- "I will never have children, so they won't have to live like this."

These promises are forged out of pain, a child's desperate attempt to make sense of a senseless world. But as they grow, these vows can harden into barriers, making it difficult to form healthy relationships or trust others.

The trauma doesn't end when the violence stops. It lingers, shaping their thoughts, behaviors, and fears. The cycle of violence continues, often mani-festing in adulthood as anxiety, depression, or even perpetuation of the same patterns they once vowed to escape.

The Unseen Scars

Rosemary learned early on how to be invisible, to hide behind the furniture, to blend into the shadows. She watched silently as her father's anger exploded, his words sharp and cruel, his hands merciless. She saw her mother cower, her spirit slowly breaking, the light in her eyes dimming with every insult, every slap, every shove.

From the corner of her room, she watched her father loom over her sister, Jean, his face contorted with rage. "Get up! Get up now, or so help me, God!" The words vibrated through the walls, shaking the floor beneath her feet. Jean tried to stand, but their father grabbed her by the hair, jerking her to her feet. "You're a liar! Born stupid, and you'll die stupid!" he spat, his grip tightening as Jean's face turned pale with fear.

Elizabeth watched, trembling, too afraid to move, too terrified to help. She covered her mouth, choking back her sobs, her tiny body shaking as she tried to disappear.

Call to Action

The cycle of violence is cruel and persistent. Without intervention, children who grow up in violent homes are more likely to enter abusive relationships as adults, either as victims or perpetrators. They learn unhealthy patterns of love and conflict resolution, repeating what they have seen because it is all they know.

Breaking this cycle requires more than just removing the child from the immediate danger. It requires understanding, compassion, and support. These children need safe spaces to express their fears and to heal from the trauma they have experienced. They need counseling to rebuild their self-esteem, to learn healthy ways of expressing emotions, and to understand that they are not to blame for the violence they have witnessed.

Chapter 3

The Role of Parents

"Parents must be proactive. They must recognize the signs of domestic violence and open the lines of communication with their children. This means listening without judgment, providing support without pressure, and helping them understand the difference between healthy and unhealthy relationships."

-Dr. Antonio R. Paiz

Educating the Next Generation

Schools, communities, and religious organizations must also play a crucial role in educating young people about healthy relationships. In a world where exposure to toxic behaviors and unhealthy relationship dynamics is increasingly common—through social media, entertainment, and even within their own homes—young people need guidance and education on what a healthy relationship truly looks like.

This education should go beyond the basics of "no means no" and delve into the foundational values of respect, self-worth, emotional intelligence, and conflict resolution. Teaching respect involves more than just being polite; it means recognizing and honoring the boundaries, autonomy, and dignity of others. It means understanding that love is not about control, jealousy, or possession, but about trust, freedom, and mutual growth.

Religious organizations, in particular, have a unique role to play. They often serve as trusted sources of guidance and support for young people. By incorporating lessons on healthy relationships, respect, and emotional intelligence into youth programs, sermons, and counseling sessions, they can help shape positive relationship values within faith-based communities.

Communities must also collaborate to provide resources and support systems for young people experiencing abuse. This includes hotlines, counseling services, legal support, and educational workshops. Schools should incorporate relationship education into their curriculums, not just as a one-time lesson but as an ongoing conversation that evolves as young people grow and encounter new challenges.

Ultimately, empowering young people to build healthy relationships requires a collective effort. It demands the involvement of schools, communities, religious organizations, parents, and peers. It requires open conversations, compassionate listening, and a commitment to breaking the cycle of abuse.

However, education alone is not enough. We must also empower young people to recognize the signs of abuse—both in their own relationships and in those around them. This includes understanding the subtle forms of manipulation, control, and emotional abuse that are often masked as love or concern. They must learn to distinguish between healthy attention and possessiveness, between caring communication and constant monitoring, and between love and control.

Developing Skills to Prevent Domestic Abuse

Conflict resolution skills are vital for maintaining healthy relationships. Disagreements are a normal part of any relationship, but it is how these conflicts are handled that determines whether the relationship is healthy or toxic. Young people must learn to communicate effectively, to listen without interrupting, to compromise without resentment, and to stand firm on their boundaries without aggression. They need to understand that disagreements should never escalate to insults, threats, or violence.

Self-worth is another essential component. Young people need to learn to value themselves, to understand that they deserve respect, love, and kindness. They must be taught that their worth is not determined by another person's approval or affection, and that they do not have to tolerate disrespect or abuse to feel loved. Building self-worth empowers them to set healthy boundaries and to walk away from toxic relationships without feeling guilt or shame.

Emotional intelligence is also crucial. Young people must learn to identify and express their emotions in healthy ways. They should be taught how to manage anger without violence, how to communicate disappointment without manipulation, and how to resolve conflicts without resorting to control or intimidation. This emotional awareness not only helps them navigate their own feelings but also fosters empathy, enabling them to recognize and respect the emotions of others.

Equally important is teaching them to set and maintain boundaries. Young people must know that it is okay to say no, to demand respect, and to leave situations that make them feel unsafe or uncomfortable. They need to be assured that setting boundaries is not selfish or rude but a fundamental aspect of self-respect and self-care.

Faith and Hope for Healing

For those trapped in abusive relationships, faith can be a source of strength and healing. "I can do all things through Christ who strengthens me." (Philippians 4:13) reminds them that they are not alone, that they are worthy of love, respect, and safety.

But faith alone is not enough. They need a community that listens, believes, and supports them without judgment. They need practical resources—hotlines, shelters, counseling, and legal protection.

Breaking free from violence is not easy. It requires courage, faith, and support. But it is possible. There is hope.

There is healing.

There is freedom.

"The light shines in the darkness, and the darkness has not overcome it."
(John 1:5)

Let us break the silence. Let us speak the truth. Let us protect our children from the shadows of abuse.

For very Erin, and every young person like her, we must stand together, in love, in faith, and in hope.

A Call to Action

We cannot afford to stay silent. Domestic violence is not just a personal issue—it's a societal crisis that affects our children, our schools, and our communities. We must raise awareness, educate young people, and empower victims to speak out. We must provide resources, support systems, and safe spaces.

Start the conversation. Use everyday moments—TV shows, news stories, social media posts—to talk about relationships, respect, and boundaries. Ask open-ended questions:

"What would you do if someone tried to control who you talked to?"

"How would you feel if someone constantly accused you of cheating without reason?"

Let them know that jealousy is not love, that possessiveness is not protection, and that control is not care. Teach them to recognize manipulation, to trust their instincts, and to know their worth.

Chapter 4

The Silent Crisis – Teen Dating Violence

"The seeds of violence are often sown in silence, watered by ignorance, and harvested in fear. To protect our children, we must be able to talk to them—even when it's uncomfortable."

-Dr. Antonio R. Paiz

The Overlooked Talk: Why Parents Must Address Dating Violence with Their Teens

Most parents are familiar with the standard conversations they need to have with their children—the talk about sex, the talk about drugs, the talk about the dangers of the adult world. But there is another conversation, just as crucial, that is often overlooked: the conversation about dating violence.

This silence isn't just an omission; it's a danger. In today's world, 1 in 3 girls experiences some form of domestic violence, often emotional or psychological, either at home or within dating relationships. These are not just statistics—they are the realities faced by our daughters, sisters, and friends. And yet, despite the prevalence of this issue, many parents find themselves unprepared to discuss it, either because they don't realize its urgency or because they simply don't know where to begin.

Dating violence isn't always physical. It often starts subtly, with controlling behavior disguised as concern, manipulation masked as affection, or constant texting and monitoring justified as love. These warning signs can be difficult to identify, especially for young people navigating their first relationships. Without guidance, they may not recognize the difference between attention and control, or between passion and possessiveness.

Parents play a pivotal role in helping their children understand what healthy relationships look like. Just as we teach them to say no to drugs or to protect themselves during sex, we must teach them to recognize the red flags of dating violence. This conversation should include more than just warnings—it should also involve discussions about respect, boundaries, and mutual trust. Our children need to know that love should never hurt, and that jealousy or control is not a sign of affection but of danger.

The consequences of ignoring this conversation can be devastating. Victims of dating violence are more likely to suffer from depression, anxiety, and other mental health issues. They are at greater risk for substance abuse, suicidal thoughts, and even continuing the cycle of violence into adulthood. By staying silent, we allow these patterns to persist.

Opening this dialogue requires vulnerability and courage, but it is essential. Parents should create a safe space for their children to ask questions, express their concerns, and share their experiences. It is important to listen without judgment, offering support and guidance rather than criticism. Empower your children with the knowledge and confidence to seek help if they ever find themselves in an unhealthy relationship.

Resources are available to help parents navigate this difficult conversation. Organizations like Loveisrespect and the National Domestic Violence Hotline offer educational materials, conversation starters, and support systems for both parents and teens. Schools and community programs may also provide workshops or counseling services.

Ultimately, the goal is not just to protect our children but to educate and empower them. By addressing dating violence head-on, we teach them to recognize their worth and to demand respect in every relationship. This is not just a conversation—it is a lifeline, a lesson in self-love and safety that every young person deserves.

A Hidden Epidemic

Dating violence is not confined to physical abuse. It is a pattern of controlling, coercive, and manipulative behaviors designed to exert power over another person. It manifests as emotional abuse, intimidation, verbal insults, isolation from friends and family, jealousy, and sometimes physical aggression.

These behaviors can be insidious, creeping in under the guise of love or protection. "I just want to spend all my time with you because I love you." "Why do you need to hang out with them when you have me?" The emotional manipulation is subtle, often disguised as affection, but it is rooted in control.

Many victims don't even realize they are being abused. They confuse jealousy with love, possessiveness with care, and isolation with protection. They rationalize the behavior because they don't know what a healthy relationship looks like.

Erin's Story: A Gradual Descent into Isolation

Erin was 19 when she met him—the boy who seemed perfect. "He'd bring me flowers just because," she recalls. In the beginning, his attention was flattering. She mistook his jealousy for love, thinking it meant he cared.

But slowly, his jealousy turned to control. He didn't just want to be with her all the time; he needed to know where she was, who she was with, and what she was doing. He became suspicious of her friends, then of her family. Eventually, he succeeded in isolating her from everyone she loved.

He never hit her, but he didn't need to. His violence was psychological—pushing her, twisting her arms, blocking the door when she tried to leave. He punched walls, screamed in her face, and made her feel small, worthless, and afraid.

When she tried to leave, he manipulated her emotions. "I love you. I need you. I'll change." And then, just as quickly, "You're nothing without me. No one will ever love you like I do."

This emotional whiplash left her confused and dependent. She started to believe him, to think that she was unworthy of love, that she was lucky to have him, even if he hurt her.

The Psychological Trap

Erin's story is painfully common. Many young people become trapped in abusive relationships because they mistake manipulation for love. They rationalize the abuse, convincing themselves that it's normal, that they deserve it, or that they can change the abuser.

Dating violence is not just about physical harm. It's about control. It's about breaking down the victim's sense of self-worth, isolating them from support systems, and creating a cycle of dependence and fear.

"I can't leave him. Who else would love me?" "It's my fault. I make him angry." "He only hurts me because he cares so much."

These thoughts are not a reflection of weakness but of manipulation. The abuser uses gaslighting, emotional abuse, and control tactics to keep the victim dependent and submissive.

The Impact on Young Lives

The impact of dating violence on young people is profound. It affects their mental health, academic performance, and social development. They may suffer from anxiety, depression, low self-esteem, and even PTSD.

They carry these wounds into adulthood, where they may struggle with trust issues, unhealthy relationship patterns, and ongoing emotional trauma. Some become abusers themselves, repeating the cycle of violence they learned as victims.

Why Not Just Leave?

One of the most common questions people ask is, "Why don't they just leave?" But the answer is complex.

Leaving an abusive relationship is terrifying. Victims fear retaliation, emotional manipulation, and social stigma. They worry that no one will believe them or that they will be blamed for the abuse.

Many victims are emotionally dependent on their abuser. They are isolated from friends and family, financially controlled, or made to believe they are unlovable.

Call to Action

The silence surrounding dating violence must end. Our young people deserve more than awareness—they deserve action, education, and empowerment. We cannot stand by while they navigate relationships without the tools to recognize manipulation, control, and abuse. It is our collective responsibility—as parents, educators, community leaders, and peers—to start these critical conversations, to teach respect, self-worth, and healthy boundaries, and to provide safe spaces where they can seek help without fear or shame.

We must leverage resources like Loveisrespect and the National Domestic Violence Hotline to support our efforts. By confronting dating violence head-on, we do more than protect our youth; we empower them to demand respect, to value themselves, and to break the cycle of violence. This is not just about ending abuse—it's about nurturing a generation that knows its worth and stands firm in its dignity. Now is the time to speak up, to educate, and to act. The safety and well-being of our children depend on it.

Chapter 5

The Hidden Grief of Leaving an Abusive Relationship

Adaptation, Practice, and Perception in the West

"Ending an abusive relationship is not just courageous; it is an act of profound loss. It is a grieving process of love that never was, grieving of dreams that will never be, and grieving the self that was shaped by abuse."

-Dr. Antonio R. Paiz

Ending an Abusive Relationship: A Journey Through Profound Loss

Whenever a relationship ends, pain follows. But the pain of leaving an abusive relationship is uniquely complex, deeply layered, and often misunderstood. It is not just the loss of a partner—it is the loss of the identity you constructed to survive, the dreams you once clung to, and the love you desperately wanted but never received.

Abusive relationships often involve a cycle of manipulation, control, and emotional dependency. Over time, the abuser systematically chips away at your sense of self, leaving you questioning your worth, your sanity, and your reality. To cope, you may have built a version of yourself that could withstand the emotional turbulence—a persona that prioritized their needs, silenced your voice, and convinced you that endurance was love. When you leave, this identity shatters, leaving you to pick up the pieces of who you were before the abuse and who you are now without them.

Even when you are the one who chooses to leave, the pain can be excruciating. You might have imagined the relief you would feel to finally be free from fear, control, and manipulation—and you do feel that relief. But with that relief comes an unexpected sorrow that can feel just as overwhelming as the abuse itself. This sorrow is not just about missing the person who hurt you; it is about mourning the person you hoped they could be.

Abusers are often skilled at alternating between cruelty and affection, creating a powerful emotional bond known as trauma bonding. This cycle of abuse and reconciliation can leave you yearning for the moments when they were kind, loving, and attentive—the moments that made you believe things would get better. Leaving means accepting that those moments were part of a manipulation strategy, not genuine love. This realization can be devastating because it means letting go of the hope that they would change, the hope that your love could save them, and the hope that the relationship could become what you once dreamed it would be.

There is also a profound sense of isolation that can accompany leaving an abusive relationship. Abusers often isolate their victims from friends and family, creating a dependency that makes leaving feel not only painful but terrifyingly lonely. You may feel as though no one understands what you went through or why you stayed for as long as you did. The shame and guilt can be suffocating, leaving you questioning your decisions, your strength, and even your sanity.

Furthermore, abusers often instill a sense of fear and helplessness that does not disappear when the relationship ends. You may continue to look over your shoulder, feel anxious about their reactions, or struggle with the psychological scars of their manipulation and control. These lingering fears can make freedom feel like a fragile illusion rather than a liberating reality.

Healing from an abusive relationship requires more than just time; it requires unlearning the lies you were made to believe, rebuilding your sense of self, and reclaiming your narrative. It involves recognizing that the pain you feel is not weakness or failure but a testament to your courage to leave and the strength it takes to rebuild.

The Complexity of Grief in Leaving Abuse

Grieving the end of an abusive relationship is complicated. It is not just about missing a person; it is about mourning the loss of a dream, an identity, and a life you hoped to build.

The sadness you feel is real, even if the relationship was toxic. It does not mean you made the wrong choice in leaving. It does not mean you should go back. It simply means you are human.

The journey is not linear. There will be days when you feel empowered and days when the grief and confusion resurface. You may find yourself missing the person who hurt you or questioning if leaving was the right choice. This is normal. Healing is a process of learning to feel safe in your own skin again, to trust your perceptions, and to believe that you are deserving of love that does not hurt.

It is crucial to seek support, whether from trusted friends, family, or professional counselors who understand the complexities of abuse. Surround yourself with people who validate your experience, remind you of your worth, and help you rebuild a life free from fear and control.

Leaving an abusive relationship is not the end of the pain, but it is the beginning of healing. It is the first step towards reclaiming your voice, your power, and your life. And although it may feel overwhelming, you are not alone. Your story matters, your pain is real, and your healing is possible.

Mourning the Loss of Intimacy

Even in abusive relationships, there are moments of tenderness, affection, and connection. The abuser is not always cruel; at times, they can be loving, attentive, and generous. These moments are not enough to justify the pain they cause, but they are enough to create emotional bonds that are difficult to break.

You may grieve the physical intimacy, the companionship, and the comfort of having someone to share your daily life with. Even if the relationship was filled with conflict and fear, there were moments of connection that felt genuine.

It's okay to miss those moments. It's okay to mourn the loss of intimacy, even when it was mixed with pain.

Losing Your Confidant

In an abusive relationship, the abuser often becomes your primary confidant—not because of trust, but because of isolation. They manipulate you into believing that no one else understands you, that no one else cares about you, and that you are nothing without them.

Even if your abuser was controlling, they were still the person you shared your thoughts, fears, and dreams with. They were the person you turned to for comfort, even when they were the source of your pain.

Leaving them means losing that confidant. It means learning to trust again, to reach out to others, and to rebuild the support network that was systematically torn apart.

Grieving Your Lost Identity

Abuse changes you. It shapes the way you see yourself, the way you see others, and the way you navigate the world. It teaches you to be cautious, to doubt your own perceptions, and to silence your voice.

After leaving an abusive relationship, many survivors feel a deep sense of loss—not just for the relationship but for the person they used to be. They grieve the loss of their confidence, their joy, and their sense of security.

You may feel like a shadow of your former self, haunted by the trauma you endured. You may struggle with anger, distrust, and fear. These are normal reactions to abnormal experiences.

The good news is that *healing is possible*. The "real you" isn't gone—it's just buried under the pain. With time, support, and self-compassion, you can rediscover who you are and rebuild the identity that was taken from you.

The Loss of Valued Possessions

Abusers often destroy cherished belongings as a way to control, punish, or manipulate their victims. You may have lost sentimental keepsakes, heirlooms, or personal items that held deep emotional value.

Leaving an abusive relationship sometimes means fleeing with nothing but the clothes on your back. You may have had to abandon a home filled with memories, possessions, and a sense of familiarity.

It's natural to grieve these losses. These items were more than just material possessions—they were symbols of your life, your history, and your identity.

Shattered Dreams and Hopes

Perhaps the most profound loss is the death of a dream. When you entered the relationship, you believed in a future—a future filled with love, companionship, and happiness. You imagined building a life together, creating a family, and growing old with someone who loved you.

Abuse shattered that dream. You may now feel disillusioned, bitter, or hopeless. You may wonder if you will ever be able to trust again, to love again, or to feel safe again.

It's okay to grieve the loss of that dream. It's okay to feel sad, angry, and heartbroken. *Your pain is real, and your dreams were valid—even if the person you dreamed them with was not.*

The Loss of Community and Connections

Leaving an abusive relationship often means losing more than just a partner. It can mean losing friends, family members, and an entire social circle. The abuser may have isolated you from loved ones, manipulated others against you, or created a narrative that made you the villain.

You may have to walk away from people who chose to believe the abuser over you. You may feel abandoned, betrayed, or utterly alone.

This is a profound loss, but it is also an opportunity. An opportunity to rebuild a community of people who genuinely care about you, who support you, and who will never betray your trust.

The Cost of Safety: Financial and Emotional Security

Leaving an abusive relationship often involves financial hardship. If your abuser controlled the finances, you may find yourself struggling to make ends meet, to rebuild your career, or to support your children.

This financial instability can trigger anxiety, fear, and a sense of helplessness. You may even find yourself questioning your decision to leave, not because you want to go back but because survival feels overwhelming.

Grieving for Your Children

If you have children with your abuser, your grief is compounded. You may feel guilt for exposing them to violence, anger for the pain they endured, and sorrow for the loss of their innocence.

You may also grieve the family you once envisioned—the dream of raising children in a loving, secure home. That dream was shattered by abuse, and it's okay to mourn that loss.

Call to Action

Grief is not a sign of weakness. It is a sign of love, hope, and humanity. It is a testament to your capacity to feel, to dream, and to care—even when those dreams were shattered and that love was betrayed.

Allow yourself to grieve. Give yourself permission to feel the sadness, the anger, and the pain. But also give yourself permission to heal.

"Blessed are those who mourn, for they will be comforted." (Matthew 5:4)

Your grief is sacred. It is a necessary step toward healing, growth, and renewal. In time, the pain will lessen, and the scars will fade. You will learn to love again, to trust again, and to dream again.

You are not broken. You are healing. And with every tear you shed, with every breath you take, you are reclaiming the life that was always yours to live.

Chapter 6

You Are Not Alone: Resources and Support

"Leaving an abusive relationship is an act of courage. It is a declaration of your worth, your strength, and your God-given right to live without fear."

-Dr. Antonio R. Paiz

Empowering Survivors Through Knowledge and Support

Knowledge is power. Understanding the justice system empowers survivors to make informed decisions, navigate complex legal landscapes, and advocate for their own safety and rights.

However, knowledge alone is not enough. Survivors need a network of support that includes legal aid, emotional counseling, community resources, and unwavering allies who will believe them and stand by their side.

Reclaiming Freedom and Navigating Justice

"With every tear you shed and every breath you take, you are reclaiming the life that was always yours to live."

Navigating the Justice System in Cases of Domestic Violence

Breaking free from domestic violence is an act of profound courage, but the journey to safety and justice is often complicated by a labyrinthine legal system.

Understanding how to navigate this system can be overwhelming, especially for survivors who are expected to grasp its complexities while battling fear, trauma, and uncertainty.

This chapter unravels the intricacies of the justice system, providing survivors, advocates, and concerned allies with a clear roadmap to pursue safety, protection, and justice. It offers insights into both the criminal and civil justice systems, outlining how each operates and how they uniquely impact domestic violence cases.

The Structure of the Justice System

The justice system is built on two main pillars: criminal law and civil law, each serving different purposes:

- Criminal Justice System: Focuses on crime and punishment, treating domestic violence as a violation against the state. This includes offenses like assault, harassment, stalking, and even homicide. Criminal cases are prosecuted by the state, not the victim, which can be both empowering and disempowering. While the state can pursue charges on behalf of the victim, the process may feel beyond the victim's control, adding to feelings of powerlessness.

- Civil Justice System: Deals with non-criminal matters, including divorce, custody disputes, property rights, and financial recovery. In domestic violence cases, civil law is often used to secure Protection Orders or Restraining Orders to safeguard victims and their children. These orders are initiated by the victim and are designed to provide safety rather than punish the abuser.

Criminal Justice System: Crime and Punishment

Criminal law addresses actions that violate penal codes, such as physical assault, harassment, stalking, and murder. These acts are prosecuted as crimes against the state to protect public safety and prevent future harm.

The state prosecutes these cases, even if the victim chooses not to press charges, ensuring accountability. This can be empowering, but it can also make survivors feel like they have lost control over the legal process.

Challenges in the Criminal Justice System:

- High Burden of Proof: To secure a conviction, the evidence must prove guilt "beyond a reasonable doubt," which can be difficult in domestic violence cases where evidence is often limited to the victim's testimony.

- Re-traumatization: Victims may feel re-victimized by having to testify against their abuser or fear retaliation if the case does not result in a conviction.

- Limited Sensitivity: The criminal justice system is not always equipped to handle the emotional complexities of domestic violence, leading to feelings of confusion, fear, and vulnerability for the survivor.

Civil Justice System: Protection and Resolution

The civil justice system provides legal remedies for personal safety, financial security, and family protection. Unlike criminal cases, civil actions are initiated by the victim, giving them more control over the process.

Types of Civil Protection Orders:

- Temporary Protection Orders (TPOs): Emergency orders providing immediate, short-term safety until a full court hearing can be held.

- Permanent Protection Orders: Long-term orders that typically last from one to five years, depending on the jurisdiction.

- No-Contact Orders: These legally prohibit the abuser from contact-

ing the victim in any form, including through third parties or elec-
tronic communication.

Advantages and Limitations of Civil Protection Orders:
- Protection Orders offer legally binding safety measures enforced by
  law enforcement, but their effectiveness relies on the abuser's willing-
  ness to comply.

- Violations can result in criminal charges, but inconsistent enforcement can leave victims feeling vulnerable.

Navigating Both Systems

Survivors often find themselves entangled in both criminal and civil legal
processes simultaneously. For example, a victim may be pursuing criminal pros-
ecution for assault while also seeking a civil Protection Order for ongoing safety
or initiating divorce and custody proceedings.

This dual navigation requires understanding different legal standards, burdens of proof, and courtroom procedures. It can be emotionally and mentally
exhausting, requiring survivors to relive traumatic experiences multiple times.

Barriers to Accessing Justice

Domestic violence survivors face numerous barriers in accessing justice, including:
- Fear of Retaliation: Abusers may threaten harm or escalate violence if
  legal action is pursued.

- Financial Constraints: Legal fees, lost income, and relocation costs can
  make pursuing justice financially challenging.

- Emotional Trauma: The psychological impact of abuse can impair
  decision-making and confidence, complicating the legal journey.

- Social Stigma and Cultural Barriers: Fear of judgment, ostracism, or cultural stigmas may discourage victims from seeking help.

- Lack of Knowledge and Support: Many survivors are unaware of their legal rights or the resources available to them.

The Role of Advocacy and Support Services

Navigating the justice system requires more than legal knowledge; it demands comprehensive support. Domestic violence advocates, legal aid organizations, and community support services are essential in guiding survivors through the legal process.

Advocates Can Help With:

- Preparing legal documents and filing Protection Orders.

- Accompanying survivors to court for emotional support.

- Connecting survivors with shelters, counseling, and financial resources.

- Educating survivors about their legal rights and empowering them to make informed decisions.

Towards a Holistic Approach to Justice

Domestic violence is more than just a legal issue; it is a public health crisis, a social justice matter, and a human rights concern. Addressing it requires a comprehensive, holistic approach that includes:

- Legal Protections: Strengthening laws that protect victims and hold abusers accountable.

- Community Education: Raising awareness about domestic violence, its signs, and its impact on society.

- Cultural Change: Challenging societal norms that perpetuate violence, control, and gender inequality.

- Support and Healing: Providing survivors with access to counseling, support groups, housing, and financial independence.

Call to Action

Ending domestic violence requires collective action:
- Community members must listen, believe, and support survivors without judgment.

- Lawmakers must create and enforce policies that protect victims and hold abusers accountable.

- Faith communities must provide compassion, guidance, and practical resources for healing.

Above all, we must break the silence. We must confront the stigma, empower survivors, and create a society where every individual can live free from violence, fear, and oppression.

Your courage reclaims your freedom. Your voice breaks the silence. Your strength rebuilds your life.

Chapter 7

Breaking the Cycle

"Together, we can make a difference. But it begins with awareness, courage, and faith."

-Dr. Antonio R. Paiz

A Faith-Based Perspective

Family violence is not just a family matter; it is a societal issue that requires a collective response. For too long, we have separated spiritual healing from practical intervention, leaving a gap in our approach to domestic violence. It is time to bridge that gap by integrating community support, legal intervention, and spiritual guidance.

Domestic violence is a complex issue that does not simply end when the abuse stops or when legal action is taken. The scars left behind are not only physical but also emotional and spiritual. Survivors often grapple with questions of worth, forgiveness, and identity, and many seek solace and healing through their faith. Yet, our current systems of support—shelters, schools, and government programs—often avoid incorporating spiritual guidance, fearing it could infringe on victims' rights or appear coercive. This well-intentioned caution, however, overlooks the profound role that faith plays in the lives of many survivors, particularly those from faith-based communities.

Through my work with the San Antonio Police Department's Family Assistance Crisis Team, I have seen the transformative power of faith in the lives of those suffering from domestic violence. I have witnessed women who, despite unimaginable pain and fear, found the strength to rebuild their lives through their spiritual beliefs. I have seen how prayer circles create safe spaces for survivors to share their stories, how pastoral counseling helps them process trauma, and how faith communities rally around victims, offering tangible support such as housing, food, and legal assistance.

Spiritual healing has the power to restore broken families, renew shattered spirits, and break the cycle of violence. For many survivors, faith is not merely a coping mechanism; it is a source of identity, hope, and resilience. By integrating spiritual guidance into our support systems, we honor the cultural and personal beliefs of survivors while providing a more holistic approach to healing.

Yet, the exclusion of spiritual support remains prevalent. In many shelters, religious symbols are removed, and discussions of faith are discouraged out of concern for maintaining a secular environment. While it is crucial to respect the diversity of beliefs among survivors, it is equally important to recognize that for some, spiritual healing is an essential part of their recovery. By avoiding this aspect, we risk alienating those who draw strength and comfort from their faith.

The solution is not to replace secular services with religious ones but to offer both, ensuring that survivors have the freedom to choose the type of support that resonates with them. This means collaborating with faith leaders who are trained in trauma-informed care, integrating spiritual counseling as an optional resource, and providing culturally sensitive support that respects each survivor's belief system.

Why the Bible?

The Bible offers timeless wisdom on love, respect, forgiveness, and reconciliation. Its teachings provide practical guidance on building healthy relationships, managing anger, and fostering compassion. It offers lessons on patience, understanding, and humility—qualities that are essential for resolving conflicts and nurturing meaningful connections. The Bible teaches that love is patient and kind (1 Corinthians 13:4-7), that respect and honor are the foundations of healthy relationships (Ephesians 5:33), and that forgiveness is a path to healing and freedom from resentment (Matthew 6:14-15).

These principles are not merely idealistic teachings; they are practical tools for building healthy, respectful, and loving relationships. For example, Ephesians 4:26-27 advises, "In your anger do not sin: Do not let the sun go down while you are still angry, and do not give the devil a foothold." This is sound advice for conflict resolution, teaching the importance of addressing issues without letting anger fester into resentment or bitterness.

The Bible also emphasizes reconciliation and restoration. In Matthew 18:15-17, Jesus provides a practical blueprint for resolving conflicts, advocating for open communication, accountability, and forgiveness. However, reconciliation is not synonymous with tolerance of abuse or harm. The Bible calls for justice and accountability, encouraging the protection of the vulnerable and the correction of wrongdoing (Isaiah 1:17, Proverbs 31:8-9).

For those who seek it, the Bible offers hope, healing, and a blueprint for rebuilding broken families. It speaks to the wounded heart, offering comfort and restoration. Psalm 147:3 says, "He heals the brokenhearted and binds up their wounds." For victims of domestic violence or broken relationships, this message can be a source of immense comfort and hope. The Bible reassures them that they are not alone, that their pain is seen, and that healing is possible.

However, this approach must be sensitive and non-coercive. It must be offered as a resource, not imposed as a requirement. It must respect individual faith journeys, cultural contexts, and personal beliefs. Not every survivor of domestic violence shares the same religious views, and for some, their abuser may have used religious teachings to justify their control or violence. Therefore, spiritual guidance must be approached with humility, sensitivity, and respect for the survivor's personal beliefs and boundaries.

Community Responsibility

Domestic violence is not just a family matter; it is a societal issue that requires a collective response. We can no longer afford to stand on the sidelines. By integrating faith-based guidance with community support and legal intervention, we can create a more holistic approach to addressing and preventing family violence.

Faith leaders and religious communities can play a pivotal role in this approach. They are often trusted figures within their communities, and their involvement can reduce the stigma associated with seeking help. However, it is crucial to educate and equip them with the tools to respond appropriately to domestic violence, avoiding victim-blaming narratives and ensuring that spiritual guidance does not replace professional counseling or legal action.

By bridging the gap between spiritual healing and practical intervention, we create a more comprehensive and inclusive support system for survivors of domestic violence. We empower them not only to escape abusive situations but also to heal emotionally, spiritually, and psychologically. We break the cycle of violence not just by addressing the physical wounds but by restoring the spirits of those who have been broken.

It is time to acknowledge that family violence is not just a family matter but a community and societal issue. It is time to recognize that for many, spiritual healing is not a luxury but a necessity. By integrating community support, legal intervention, and spiritual guidance, we can provide survivors with the holistic healing they deserve.

Call to Action

It is crucial to collaborate with faith leaders who are trauma-informed and who understand the complexities of domestic violence. Religious communities can provide safe spaces for healing, but they must also be careful not to pressure survivors into premature forgiveness or reconciliation. Forgiveness is a personal journey, and while it can be a powerful tool for healing, it should never be used to justify continued abuse or to dismiss the need for justice and accountability.

As written in Matthew 11:28, "Come unto me, all ye that labor and are heavy laden, and I will give you rest." This message of hope and healing is powerful, and for many, it is a crucial element in their journey to recovery. For survivors, it offers a refuge—a place of rest from the emotional, psychological, and spiritual burdens they carry. It is an invitation to lay down the weight of shame, fear, and pain, and to find peace in faith.

Ultimately, integrating spiritual guidance with practical intervention provides a holistic approach to healing. It addresses not only the emotional and physical wounds but also the spiritual scars left by abuse. By offering faith as a resource rather than a requirement, we empower survivors to reclaim their narratives, to heal in their own way, and to rebuild their lives with dignity and hope.

Chapter 8

Conclusion

Biblical Guidance for Building Healthy
Relationships and Ending Domestic Violence

"Breaking the cycle of domestic violence requires more than legal intervention or community awareness. It requires healing. For many, that healing comes from faith, from finding hope and purpose through spiritual guidance."

-Dr. Antonio R. Paiz

Faith, Justice, and Healing

The Bible offers not only hope but also practical guidance for building healthier relationships. It teaches love, respect, and forgiveness. But it also teaches strength, courage, and justice. Using faith as a tool for healing does not mean ignoring the need for accountability or justice. Instead, it offers a pathway to forgiveness and rebuilding, for both victims and perpetrators.

One of the most profound aspects of biblical teaching is its emphasis on love and respect. In Ephesians 5:25, husbands are instructed to "love your wives, just as Christ loved the church and gave himself up for her." This love is not about control or domination; it is about sacrifice, protection, and nurturing. It is about putting the well-being of one's partner above selfish desires. This foundation of respect and care is crucial for building healthy relationships, free from abuse and manipulation.

At the same time, the Bible emphasizes the importance of justice and accountability. In Isaiah 1:17, believers are called to "seek justice, correct oppression; bring justice to the fatherless, plead the widow's cause." This directive makes it clear that faith is not about passive endurance but about actively challenging injustice and protecting the vulnerable. For victims of domestic violence, this means that seeking justice is not only acceptable but also a godly act of self-respect and courage.

Forgiveness is another cornerstone of biblical teaching, often misunderstood as excusing or tolerating harm. In reality, forgiveness, as taught by Christ, is about freeing oneself from bitterness and resentment, not about condoning abusive behavior. In Matthew 18:21-22, Jesus teaches about forgiveness, but this does not mean ignoring accountability. Forgiveness is a personal journey of healing, allowing victims to reclaim their peace, but it does not require them to continue a relationship with their abuser.

In fact, the Bible acknowledges the importance of setting boundaries for self-preservation. In Proverbs 22:24-25, it says, "Do not make friends with a hot-tempered person, do not associate with one easily angered, or you may learn their ways and get yourself ensnared." This wisdom highlights the necessity of distancing oneself from toxic influences, including abusive partners.

The Bible also empowers victims with the courage to seek help and justice. In Psalm 82:3-4, it says, "Defend the weak and the fatherless; uphold the cause of the poor and the oppressed. Rescue the weak and the needy; deliver them from the hand of the wicked." This is a call to action, not just for faith communities but for survivors themselves, encouraging them to seek safety and justice without shame.

For perpetrators of abuse, the Bible offers a pathway to repentance and transformation. In Ezekiel 18:30-32, God calls for repentance and a change of heart: "Repent! Turn away from all your offenses; then sin will not be your downfall. Rid yourselves of all the offenses you have committed, and get a new heart and a new spirit." This means that true repentance requires accountability, restitution, and genuine change, not just apologies.

We cannot stand on the sidelines while children grow up in homes filled with anger, fear, and violence. It is our responsibility—as parents, neighbors, teachers, and community leaders—to protect the innocent, to break the cycle, to speak up.

We must acknowledge the problem, educate ourselves and others, and create safe spaces where victims can find support and healing. Religious leaders and communities of faith must work together to provide resources, counseling, and spiritual guidance, creating a bridge between faith and practical support.

The Power of Hope and Healing

The cycle of violence can be broken. Children like Rosemary and Elizabeth don't have to grow up to repeat the patterns they witnessed. Through faith, community support, and a commitment to change, we can create a world where children grow up feeling safe, loved, and free from fear.

But it begins with us. It begins with courage, compassion, and the unwavering belief that every child deserves a life free from violence.

The verse, "Come unto me, all ye that labor and are heavy laden, and I will give you rest" (Matthew 11:28), speaks directly to those burdened by pain, fear, and guilt. For victims, it is an invitation to find solace, healing, and rest in God's love. For perpetrators seeking redemption, it is an invitation to confront their actions, seek forgiveness, and transform their hearts.

Using faith as a tool for healing does not mean ignoring justice; it means balancing justice with compassion, accountability with forgiveness, and truth with love. It means empowering survivors to reclaim their dignity and helping perpetrators to confront their actions and seek true transformation. By integrating biblical principles with practical intervention, we can build healthier, more loving relationships grounded in respect, justice, and grace.

There is hope.

There is healing.

And in the name of Jesus, there is victory over fear and pain.

Bibliography

1. Browne, Angela. When Battered Women Kill and Living with the Enemy. New York: Free Press, 1987, pp. 34.

2. Buzawa, E.S., and Buzawa, C.G. Approaches to Domestic Violence: The Criminal Justice Response. Sage Publications, Thousand Oaks, CA, 1996, pp. 76-77.

3. Burby, Liza N. Protect the Well-Being of the Family. Family Violence. Library of Congress Cataloging in Publication, 1996, pp. 27.

4. Bishops, Permanent Council on Violence Against Women. Live Without Fear. Austin, TX: Publication, June 13, 1991, pp. 7.

5. Dugan, M., and Hock, R. It's My Life Now. New York: Routledge, 2000.

6. Gondolf, Edward W. Assessing Women Battering in Mental Health Services. Sage Publications, 1998, pp. 68.

7. Greenberg, Keith. Family Abuse. Fitzhenry & Whiteside Ltd, Markham, Ontario, 1998, pp. 15.

8. Hong, Maria. Asian American: An Anthology. Selected as one of the best books for teenagers. Rosen Publishing Group, New York, NY, 1997.

9. McEvoy, A.W., Brookings, J., and Holmes, B. Help Battered Women: A Volunteer's Handbook for Assisting Victims of Marital Violence. Learning Publications, Holmes Beach, FL, 1982, pp. 135.

10. Rinch, E. Jamice. Family Violence. Lerner Publications Company, Minneapolis, MN, 1992, pp. 15-16.

11. Roleff, Tamara L. Domestic Violence: Family Violence. Library of Congress Cataloging-Public Data, 1959, pp. 15.

12. Wolfe, Jaffe, P.G., and Wilson, S.K., D.A. Children of Battered Women. Sage Publications, Newbury Park, CA, 1990, pp. 22-42.